Santa in a Snow Globe

By AH Edelman

Illustrated by Serge Gall

© 2020 A.H. Edelman

All rights reserved. No part of this book may be reproduced, stored in a retrieval system, or transmitted in any form, by any means, including mechanical, electronic, photocopying, recording, or otherwise without the prior written consent of the publisher.

Paperback: 978-0-9908871-4-0

eBook: 978-0-9908871-6-4

Hardback: 978-0-9908871-8-8

Published by IndieReader
Story by AH Edelman
Illustrations by Serge Gall

AH Edelman is the author of *The Little Black Dress* and *Manless in Montclair*. And, yes, she still believes in Santa.

Serge Srećko Gall, originally from Zagreb, Croatia, is a painter and illustrator whose work has appeared in publications including *The New York Times*, *Esquire*, and *The New Yorker*. He lives in Hillsdale, NY and is currently working on his autobiographical graphic novel.

AH Edelman
For my family, who give me endless love and support,
and for Santa and the magic of Christmas,
which continue to give me hope.

Serge Gall
Dedicated to children everywhere.

ACKNOWLEDGMENTS

This book would not have been possible without the
help, advice, and support from the following:
Phil Leo, Tata and Mirjana Gall, Ed Charlton, Grace Spampinato,
Andie Chalfant, the Edelman girls, Rion Dugan
and
Santa Stephen Arnold for the inspiration.

'Twas the week before Christmas
and all through the store,
the lights gently glimmered
like knobs on a door.

Most people wore masks
and stood six feet apart,
but it was the week before Christmas
so they did it with heart.

They were there for one reason,
the parents and kids,
the teens with their cell phones,
the babies with bibs.

They were waiting for Santa,
hoping he'd grant them a wish,
a new bike for Michael,
a skateboard for Trish.

So they searched and they searched
until Santa was found,
enclosed in a place
that was clear and quite round.

Why is he in there,
children wanted to know.

Why was he sitting
in a globe filled with snow?

"I'll tell you the reason,"
said an elf standing nearby.

"He's no longer young
and he still has to fly.

He's doing his part
to keep people safe.

And let us be honest,
that *is* Santa's way."

"But what about Christmas?"
anxiously asked a small boy.

"Was I good for no reason
if there aren't any toys?"

The elf waved him forward
to stand by the glass.

"Is it true," he asked Santa,
"this year won't be like last?"

Santa thought for a moment
before starting to speak.

A rosy glow spread
from his ears to his cheeks.

"The one thing that's constant is change,"
he declared.

"And sometimes that's frightening,
but there's no need to be scared."

"The truth is our planet
is not in great shape.

There's been fighting and sickness
and fires untamed.

As for my coming,
we're preparing the sled.

We'll arrive, just like last year,
after you've gone to bed."

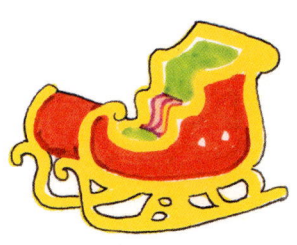

"So then," said the boy,
 "I guess things are all good.

I'll get all my presents
 like you promised I would."

But Santa leaned back,
 concern clear on his face;
 there was a lesson to share
 about compassion and grace.

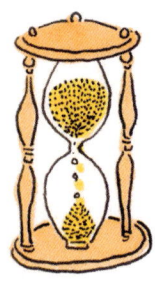

Sell your books at sellbackyourBook.com!
Go to sellbackyourBook.com and get an instant price quote. We even pay the shipping - see what your old books are worth today!

Inspected By: veronica_nunez

0004036२४18

"I'm not out that often
but I see things aren't right.

The North Pole is warmer;
species disappear overnight."

The child looked confused;
he had not understood.

So Santa took another tack;
it was important that he should.

"I'll tell you a secret,
   it's not just about stuff.

It's being thankful for the little things
and smiling when it's tough.

It's about sharing what you have
with those who may have less.

It's not measuring worth in money
to determine who is best."

"You see our world is like a snow globe,
round and fragile to the touch.

And when the snow is falling,
it's hard to see too much.

But when everything has cleared,
its time to do our best.

To help out who, and when, we can
is a very worthy quest."

"We're all in this together,
underneath the same big sky.

We're made of stars and special stuff,
not apparent to the eye.

Christmas season is upon us;
we must remember what that means.

Kindness, above all else,
is what our planet needs."

The little boy nodded slowly,
understanding dawning slow.

It doesn't matter how long it takes;
it matters which way you go.

So they smiled for a picture,
the child moving toward the door.

We're truly all connected.
Of that, you can be sure.

After all, thought Santa smiling,
Christmas has always been the season
for miracles and hope, which—let's face it—
have little to do with reason.

So don't be too concerned if this year
Santa can be found,
sitting in a snow globe
that is as clear as it is round.

Made in the USA
Monee, IL
14 November 2020